Making a R

John Boakes

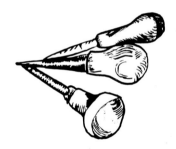

Smith
Settle

First published in 2001 by
Smith Settle Ltd
Ilkley Road
Otley
West Yorkshire
LS21 3JP

© John Boakes 2001

All rights reserved. No part of this book may be reproduced, stored or introduced into
a retrieval system, or transmitted in any form or by any means (electronic, mechanical,
photocopying, recording or otherwise) without the prior permission of Smith Settle Ltd.

The right of John Boakes to be identified as the author of this work has been asserted
by him in accordance with the Copyright, Designs and Patents Act 1988.

ISBN 1 85825 116 8

British Library Cataloguing-in-Publication data:
A catalogue record for this book is available from the British Library.

Set in Monotype Plantin

Designed, printed and bound by
SMITH SETTLE
Ilkley Road, Otley, West Yorkshire LS21 3JP

Introduction

The craft of making *rag rugs* is worldwide, and probably dates from around 2000 BC. This particular way of making rugs first came to Great Britain, and to Scotland in particular, around the late 1400s. First seen in Scotland, knowledge and skill in the making of these rugs was very slow in spreading throughout the country. The rugs were only made by poor itinerant women, called *rag rug women*, who travelled from community to community and island to island making a rug for anybody who would give them a small payment of money as well as food and board in return. Thus it took a long time for the skills that these women possessed to gradually pass through all of Scotland and subsequently into England. This form of payment and barter actually continued in the remoter parts of Scotland well into the twentieth century.

The skill in the making of these rugs finally came to the North of England around late Tudor times, and lasted for centuries. Even within living memory there was an itinerant rug man travelling around the Yorkshire Dales making rugs, much like the rag rug women of Scotland many hundreds of years before. Unfortunately very few examples of these early rugs have survived. The rugs were regarded as an everyday item, and were used until they were completely threadbare and worn out, before being disposed of.

The ease of making of these rag rugs as well as the use of readily obtainable materials made them very cheap and therefore very popular as time went on. This popularity and cheapness eventually meant that they became synonymous with the working classes all over the country, and the North of England in particular. Rugs made in the northern counties varied slightly from those made in the rest of the country by using strips of material cut into two inches (50mm) long by one inch (25mm) wide instead of the four inches (100mm) long by two inches (50mm) wide usually used elsewhere. Rugs were made from any old or discarded material. When enough had been collected — and it would take up to 20 lbs (8kg) of old clothes, curtains and blankets — it then was cut up to give a quantity of usable pieces. These were then cut into strips of the correct size, before finally being worked into a backing of any coarsely woven cloth; in some cases this was an old clean hessian sack or perhaps even a larger sugar sack. Rag rugs were made and used in households all over England, but it was in the North in particular that they were to become the most popular and widely used. Here the textile mills and factories were an important part of life by not only providing employment for large numbers of workers, but also by producing vast amounts of waste material that could be easily recycled and used in the making of rag rugs.

The rag rug has been called by many local names all over England. In Yorkshire it was usually called a *proddie* rug or *peggie* rug. But in other parts of the country this same rag rug has also been called a *hooky*, *proggy*, *clippy* or *bodgy* rug. A recent count of such different names for this ubiquitous rug from all over the country has given a total of seventeen.

In the working class home, rag rug making was a family pastime, and it would take up to sixty hours to complete a fireside rug. The man of the house would make the frame for holding the rug taut while it was being made, as well as the *prodders*. These were simple tools made from either broken keys, dolly pegs or knives and forks, which were shaped at one end so that they were easy to hold and had a blunt point on the other with which to work the strips. His wife would do the rug making, as well as choosing the mix of colours from what was available and the pattern to be used. The children were not left out, for they were responsible for cutting the material into the required sized strips.

Because the patterns and colours of these rugs could be seen on both sides, they were reversible. The finished articles therefore usually spent a lot of the time being used upside-down during the week. Normally they were only placed right side up when visitors came. This practice made them last longer and ensured that they lasted in a good state of repair for as long as possible.

Rag rug making was a continual part of the household life, and when a rug was finished it was not unusual to begin a new one straight away. A newly finished one would be given pride of place in front of the fire in the the main room of the house. The older, more worn rugs would be moved around to the lesser rooms of the house, and finally when they were nearly worn out, they finished their life outside the back door or even in the outside 'nessy' or toilet.

In lonely country villages, where community life was limited, it was not unusual for groups of women to get together in each other's homes to make rugs. These rugs often depicted local scenes or events of importance, and when they were finished they would either be given to their local church or chapel, who in turn sold them for the church funds or else gave them to the poor of the district. This practice has lasted in some areas until the present day, with the Arkengarthdale Prodders of Yorkshire being a fine example. Over the years these ladies have made and sold many rugs to help their local chapel funds in Langthwaite.

Heather Ritchie is another rag rug-maker from the Yorkshire Dales area. Her thriving workshop is in the heart of beautiful Swaledale, where she not only makes rugs to sell, but also holds workshops for children and adults alike so that she can pass on the traditional skills to even more people. Heather has gained her twenty-five years of knowledge not only from other rag rug-makers in this country, but by travelling all over the world and to America in particular, where she is often asked to give teaching courses to the rag rug-makers there. In the latter part of this book she shows the steps in which a rag rug is made, using the traditional methods going back hundreds of years.

Bibliography

Ann Davis, *Rag Rugs* (1992).
Alison Jenkins, *Traditional Country Crafts* (nd).
W W Kent, *The Hooked Rug* (1930).

Acknowledgements

The author would like to thank: Heather Ritchie, rug-maker, of Reeth in the Yorkshire Dales; Nicola Mills of the Beamish Photographic Library for the use of the photographs on pages 8-12 and 13 (left) and Caroline Benson of the Rural History Centre at Reading University for the photo on page 13 (right).

The very different finished effects of a variety of rag rugs. The one on the right is of a woven Turkish-style rug, the next a hooked rug; in the centre is a plaited one, then a *clippy* rag rug, whilst that on the left is another plaited one.

Two ladies in 1910 making a clippy mat outdoors in Hexham.

Rug making at Consett Boys' Club, 1937.

Two members of the same family rug making. (Two different photographs of the same scene have been mounted side by side.)

Rug making at home in the early 1900s.

A group of ladies rug making outdoors in the 1920s as they display their finished work to the camera.

(Left) Proggy rug making in the yard of what looks like an old terraced house.
(Right) An old lady takes in the sun whilst she makes an oval rag rug.

A pile of old clothes and rugs in Heather Ritchie's studio in the Yorkshire Dales, waiting to be cut into usable strips to make into a rag rug.

The pieces used to be cut into strips by hand with a pair of scissors or a sharp knife. In the past, a matchbox was used as a template to make the correct-sized strips.

Nowadays Heather can use modern-day cutters. *(Top)* A piece of material is fed into the machine. *(Bottom)* The handle is turned and the material is cut into strips as it is fed through the machine.

In the past, the backing for rag rugs was usually a piece of old sacking which had been washed, such as those in this picture.

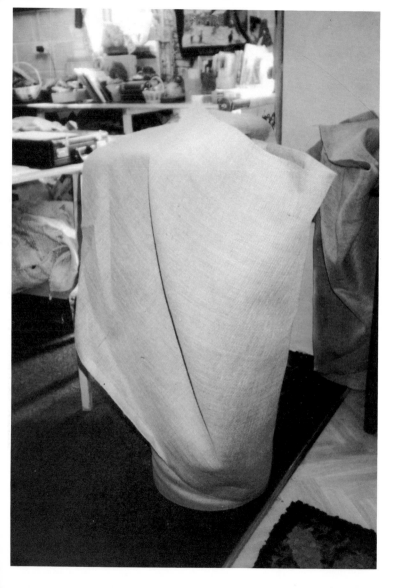

Nowadays it is usual to buy specially made burlap for the backing. Heather purchases her burlap from mills in Scotland.

The burlap is cut to size and fixed on to the frame. Here we can see how the backing is secured.

The pattern is marked out. On a small rug, this would have been marked out all at once. But here we can see that Heather is working on a large rug and is marking out a piece at a time.

Working from the back, a hole is made in the burlap with the prodder.
Then the strips are pushed through from behind.

The strip is pulled through from underneath by the other hand. Then another hole is made and the other end of the strip is pushed down through this. This process continues until all the backing is completely covered.

In this photograph, Heather is about to pull the strip tight.

To make the pattern, Heather uses the same coloured strips in blocks. As the rug proceeds, not only should the work be tight, but there shouldn't be any hessian showing once the rug is finished.

Another colour is about to be started.

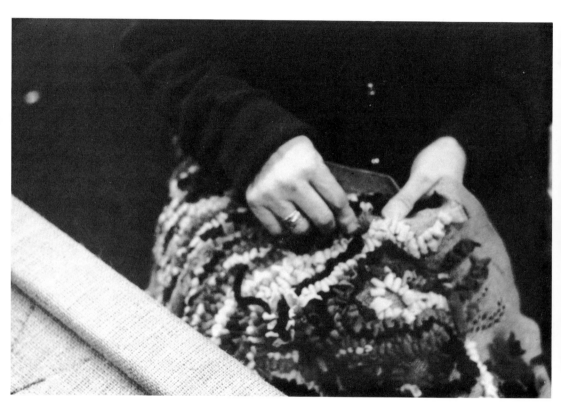

In the past, if there wasn't a frame on which to stretch the rug as they worked, the women used to work the loose rug on their knees as they sat by the fire. Here Heather uses an antique prodder.

Sometimes Heather has to dye the material before use. Here are the many different colours she utilises. Heather uses only natural dyes.

A selection of antique prodders. The one at the front on the left is made from a broken key.

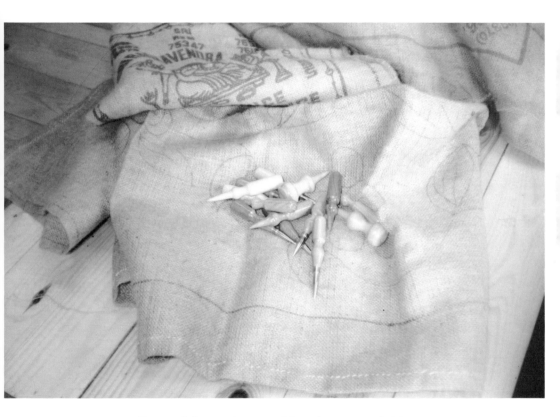

Some of the modern prodders that are available.

A selection of old hand 'speed' prodders.

This photograph shows how the 'speed' prodders worked. One half of the prodder is held in one hand, whilst the other hand moved the other half up and down on a strip of material to work it into the backing.

Since the Second World War, there have been many different aids to rag rug-making. This is a 1950s Airlyne automatic rug machine.

Once the Airlyne had been attached to the edge of a table, it was operated by a strap that fitted over the foot. When this was worked up and down, it enabled the prodding arm, which is attached to a spring, to work. If not used carefully, this could be a very dangerous machine. One wonders if it would pass the safety standards of today.

Heather also makes picture rag rugs, and for this she sometimes uses wool. Here, hanks of dyed wool are hung up to dry.

Baskets of ready-cut strips waiting to be used.

Three antique hooky rugs.

A half-finished clippy rag rug. The modern frame that is holding the rug has not altered in design for many centuries.

The traditional finished look of another clippy rag rug.

A half-finished hooky rug. This was made as a community effort for the Millennium by the people of Reeth in the Yorkshire Dales.

Here we can see some of the Reeth villagers working on the village Millennium rug.

The different look of a finished *lambs' lugs* rag rug. This type of rug is usually made only from cotton material. The points are meant to represent young lambs' ears, and a great number of these rugs were made in the Bowes area of County Durham by groups of ladies not unlike the Arkengarthdale Prodders of the Yorkshire Dales.

A selection of picture rugs hanging in Heather's workshop. The majority of these rugs are made entirely from wool.

A close-up of one of the rugs opposite, 'The Reeth Parliament'. This shows the amount of detail that can be achieved by an expert rug-maker.

This is another of Heather's rugs, showing a picture of Reeth.

This is the finished look of a realistically hooked rug depicting a Swaledale sheep. It is made from strips of woollen material, some of it specially dyed.

DALES COUNTRYSIDE MUSEUM

1999

(Right) Heather works on another rag rug.

(Facing page) One of Heather's commissions was a large, realistic rag rug for the Dales Countryside Museum in Hawes. Here the finished rug awaits delivery.